Sa+L

THE RHYME BIBLE ACTIVITY BOOK

published by Gold'n'Honey Books
a part of the Questar publishing family

© 1997 by L. J. Sattgast

Illustrations © 1997 by Toni Goffe

International Standard Book Number: 1-57673-050-6

Design by D² DesignWorks

Printed in the United States of America

For information:
QUESTAR PUBLISHERS, INC.
POST OFFICE BOX 1720
SISTERS, OREGON 97759

Library of Congress Cataloging-in-Publication Data:

Sattgast, L. J., 1953-
     The rhyme Bible activity book / by L. J. Sattgast ; illustrated by Toni Goffe.
          p.   cm.
Summary: This companion to The rhyme Bible includes projects such as
tongue twisters, puzzles, and mind bogglers.
     ISBN 1-57673-050-6 (alk. paper)
     1. Bible games and puzzles--Juvenile literature. 2. Bible--Miscellanea--Juvenile literature.
  [1. Bible games and puzzles. 2. Bible--Miscellanea.]   I. Goffe, Toni, ill.   II. Title.
GV1507.B5s28   1997
220--dc21   96-51530
                                                        CIP
                                                         AC

     97 98 99 00 01 — 10 9 8 7 6 5 4 3 2 1

The Rhyme Bible

Activity Book

TEXT BY L. J. SATTGAST
ILLUSTRATIONS BY TONI GOFFE

Gold 'n' Honey
BOOKS

S I S T E R S ,   O R E G O N

Matching Tails

God made everything
Perfect and good,
But things don't look
The way they should!
Find each tail—
short or long;
It seems the artist
Got them wrong!
So match each tail
That's out of place,
And make it fit
The animal face!

(If you need to look,
the answers are on page 60.)

6

Fruit Basket

The Garden of Eden
Had beautiful trees
With wonderful fruit
Among the leaves.
Match each tree
With the word below
That tells what kind
Of fruit it grows.

coconut

apple

orange   cherry   lemon   pear   banana

Animal Riddles

God brought animals
To the boat.
He brought some cows
And sheep and goats.
Lions and tigers
And zebras came,
So match the riddle
To the name!

I do not like
To see a cat.
I nibble cheese,
I am a —

I'm not too small
And not too big.
I like to eat,
I am a —

I have big claws
And lots of hair.
I stand up tall,
I am a —

I'm very happy
In a bog.
I sit and croak,
I am a —

I only grin;
I never laugh.
My neck is long,
I'm a —

Heavenly Dreams

Joseph had strange dreams
As he lay upon his cot.
Which of these were in his dreams,
And which of them were not?

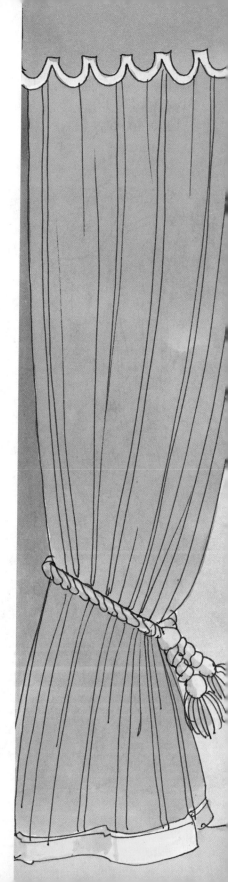

Hidden Pictures

The princess came
To take a bath
In the River Nile,
But what she found
Among the reeds
Made the princess smile.

Some other things
Are hiding there
That aren't as plain to see,
But if you look
You'll find them all,
From book to bumblebee!

Fun With Frogs

Frogs jumping here,
Frogs jumping there,
Down on the ground
And up in the air!

How many frogs
Are leaping about
And making the king
Holler and shout?

Look Alikes

God told the people
To march to Jericho.
He said, "You must be quiet
Till you hear
The trumpet blow!"
Six of the priests
Are ready for the shout,
But only two are just alike—
Can you pick them out?

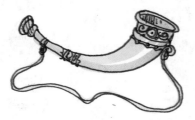

A

D

B

C

E

F

Search and Find

Goliath had a sword and spear,
And David had a sling.
But God would help him
Win the fight
And someday make him king.
And now it's time
For you to look,
If you are so inclined,
At all the things
We've pictured here
For you to search and find!

harp   spoon

lizard   kite   sword   book   sailboat

Out of Order!

The story of Elijah
Is such a mixed-up mess!
It's hard to tell
What's happening;
You simply have to guess.
But since you are so clever,
Let's see if you can fix
The crazy mixed-up order
Of pictures one through six!

1

4

2

3

5

6

Old & New

Jonah ran away from God
And went aboard a ship.
It wasn't long before he took
An unexpected trip!
Many things are pictured here
And most of them belong,
But some were not
Invented yet,
So which of them are wrong?

Rhyme Swap

Something is wacky.
These verses don't rhyme,
Look at each ending–
It's wrong every time!

So carefully look
And see what is wrong,
And then find the place
Where the endings belong!

1.

Daniel was faithful
Three times a day.
He got on his knees
And started to... lunch.

2.

An angel will often
Have something to say.
But this angel came
To keep lions... right!

3.

The lions were hungry.
They wanted to munch,
But none of them dared
To eat Daniel for... pray!

4.

The king had worried
All through the night.
He yelled down to Daniel,
"I hope you're all... away!"

Stable Sounds

Little Baby Jesus
Was born in a stable,
So try to match,
If you are able,
Some sounds that Jesus
May have heard
With the right creature—
Animal or bird!

Meow!   Moo!

Woof!   Ba-a-a-a!   Hee! Haw!   Coo! Coo!   Squeak!

Alphabet Math

Some shepherds were out
In a field one night
When all of a sudden,
They saw a light!
So do your math
And if you're right,
You'll spell four things
They saw that night.

(Hint: Always work
From left to right!)

shell + beep − bell =

ant + go + helps − pot − h =

man + tiger − it =

bat + boy − to =

Starry Night

Twinkle, twinkle special star,
How we wonder what you are,
Up above the world so high,
Like a diamond in the sky.
We will travel very far
Following this special star!

Now let's see
How good you are
At counting every single star!

Search & Find II

Jesus was lost!
He couldn't be found
Though Mary and Joseph
Looked all around.
Try to find him
And when you do,
Then try to find
His parents too!

Now please look,
If you don't mind,
And see how many
Scrolls you find!

Jesus

Mary & Joseph

Scroll
(The Bible)

Finish
the Rhyme

Jesus walked
From town to town
Preaching every day.
And people listened eagerly
To all he had to say.
Read the things
That Jesus taught
And guess the words
That rhyme.
The pictures on the other page
Will help you every time!

1. You are like
A shining...
If you learn
To do what's right.

2. The road to God
Is small and straight,
And few will enter
Through the...

3. Please be kind
To one another.
Don't be angry
With your...

4. Flowers do not
Work or...
Yet the Father
Helps them grow.

5. Don't store treasure
Here on...
It will rust
And lose its worth.

6. It's been said,
'A tooth for a...'
But kindness is
A better truth!

Out of Order II

Jesus healed a man
Who was lowered
Through the roof.
But something's
Out of order here—
I think the artist goofed!

So if you know
What it's about,
Then try to sort
The story out,
And when you're done
I'm sure you'll know
The order that
The pictures go.

A

D

B

C

E

F

Who Said It?

Read the things
That people said
When Jairus' daughter
Was sick in bed.
Can you tell
Who said each one?
Give it a try
And have some fun!

The Servant

Jesus   Jairus' Daughter   Jairus

Hunt & Count

My, what a crowd!
They look well fed,
For Jesus has given them
Fish and bread.
After they passed
The food around,
Twelve baskets full
Could still be found.
Look for the baskets
And then find the lad
Who shared with Jesus
All that he had!

Tools of the Trade

A wise man builds
On solid land.
A foolish one builds
Upon the sand.
Pretend you built
A house today.
Look at the tools
On display.
Pick the tools
That you would use.
Then list the ones
You wouldn't choose!

Match-up

Jesus told us
To love one another.
He said to be kind
To our sisters and brothers.
Here are some people
Who often say,
"Let me help you,
If I may!"
Look at the objects
That they might use.
And see if you know
Which one they would choose.

Treasure Hunt

How the rich man
Loves his treasure!
He counts it and hides it,
And feels such pleasure!
But if you look
You'll find, I'm told—
Ten silver coins
And five bags of gold!

Which Way?

Look at this boy—
He's hungry and sad!
He wants to go home
To be with his dad.
Help him to find
The road that is right
So he can be home
With his father tonight!

Finish Here

Start Here

Secret Code

Crack the code
And you will know
What Jesus said
So long ago!

(Psssst!—Find the letter in the code
and match it to the one below!)

A B C D E F G H I
| | | | | | | | |
Z Y X W V U T S R

J K L M N O P Q
| | | | | | | |
Q P O N M L K J

R S T U V U X Y Z
| | | | | | | | |
I H G F E D C B A

Memory Whiz!

Little Zacchaeus
Climbed up a tree.
When he looked down,
What did he see?
Study the picture
A minute or three,
Then cover it up
So you cannot see.
Next you can answer
Each question below.
(But first turn the book
So the questions will show!)

6. What was the hungry donkey chewing?
5. What were some naughty children doing?
4. How many dogs were running around?
3. What was falling to the ground?
2. How many birds were in the tree?
1. How many chickens did you see?

Hidden Hearts

A heart means love,
And love is why
Our Savior, Jesus,
Came to die.
He died to take
Our sins away
So we could live
With him someday.
Carefully look
Inside the square
And find each heart
That's hidden there!

For God so loved the world
that he gave his one and only Son,
that whoever believes in him
shall not perish but have eternal life.

JOHN 3:16

Rhyme Riddles

One Sunday morning,
Before the break of day,
God did a miracle,
We celebrate today!

So read the rhyming riddles,
And tell me if you know,
Who was there that Easter day
So very long ago?

1.
I died upon a cross
And was buried in a tomb,
But when the women came to see
They found an empty room!
Who am I?

2.
I came on Sunday morning
Before the light of day.
It wasn't very hard for me
To roll the stone away!
Who am I?

3.
Such news the women brought us!
We ran at once to see.
But at the tomb we wondered,
Where could Jesus be?
Who are we?

4.
I thought he was the gardener
For tears had filled my eyes.
When Jesus called me by my name
Imagine my surprise!
Who am I?

The Rhyme Bible Activity Book Answers

MATCHING TAILS - PAGE 28

This animal's tail . . . should be on this animal:

lion	beaver
pig	fox
beaver	elephant
cat	pig
elephant	cat
fox	fish
fish	mouse
mouse	monkey
parrot	lion
monkey	parrot

ANIMAL RIDDLES-PAGE 10

A. rat
B. pig
C. bear
D. frog
E. giraffe

HEAVENLY DREAMS-PAGE 12

YES
sheaf of wheat
sun
moon
stars

NO
rainbow
flower
waterpot
cloud
scroll
pumpkin
teddy bear

FUN WITH FROGS-PAGE 16

We counted 45

LOOK ALIKES - PAGE 18

A and E

SEARCH AND FIND - PAGE 20

harp in left tree
spoon on soldier's spear
lizard on lower right rocks
kite in right tree
dagger in left tree
book under soldier's arm
sailboat in left tree

OUT OF ORDER!

4
1
6
3
5
2

OLD & NEW - PAGE 24

airplane
submarine
tie and socks
briefcase
watch
cell phone
paratrooper
helicopter

RHYME SWAP - PAGE 26

1. pray instead of lunch
2. away instead of right
3. lunch instead of pray
4. right instead of away

STABLE SOUNDS - PAGE 28

meow - cat
moo - cow
woof - dog
Baa - sheep
heehaw - donkey
coo coo - dove
squeak - mouse

ALPHABET MATH - PAGE 30

1. sheep
2. angels
3. manger
4. baby

STARRY NIGHT - PAGE 32

99 stars in the sky
If you count the star on the left
you have 100!

SEARCH & FIND II - PAGE 34

Jesus in lower right corner.
Mary and Joseph on lower right rooftop.
There are 10 scrolls

FINISH THE RHYME - PAGE 36

1. light
2. gate
3. brother
4. sew
5. earth
6. tooth

OUT OF ORDER II - PAGE 38

C
F
A
E
B
D

WHO SAID IT? - PAGE 40

A — Jairus
B — Jairus
C — Jesus
D — The Servant
E — Jesus
F — Jesus

HUNT AND COUNT - PAGE 42

12 baskets

TOOLS OF THE TRADE - PAGE 44

Tools to use:
hammer
saw
nails
drill
ladder

Tools not to use:
electric beater
tea pot
toaster
fan
pot

MATCH-UP - PAGE 46

Fireman — fire hydrant
Chef — platter of food
Nurse — stethoscope
Policeman — night stick
Ice cream man — ice cream cone

TREASURE HUNT - PAGE 48

3 bags of gold in trees
2 bags in lower left

SECRET CODE - PAGE 52

"Let the children come to me!"

MEMORY WHIZ! - PAGE 54

1. Seven chickens
2. Five birds (one chicken)
3. Bananas from a basket
4. Four dogs
5. Stealing fruit
6. Flowers

HIDDEN HEARTS - PAGE 56

56 hearts

RHYME RIDDLES - PAGE 58

1. Jesus
2. angel
3. Peter & John
4. Mary